Jack Ma
In His Own Words

Jack Ma
In His Own Words

EDITED BY
SUK LEE
AND
BOB SONG

AN AGATE IMPRINT
CHICAGO

The first edition of this book was published in 2016 under the title *Never Give Up*. This edition has been updated and expanded.

Printed in the United States of America

10 9 8 7 6 5 4 3 2 1   19 20 21 22 23

ISBN-13: 978-1-57284-264-9
ISBN-10: 1-57284-264-4

The Library of Congress has cataloged a previous edition of this book as follows:

Names: Lee, Suk (Freelance editor), editor. | Ma, Yun, 1964 - contributor.
Title: Never give up : Jack Ma in his own words / edited by Suk Lee and Bob Song.
Description: Chicago : Agate/B2, [2016] | Series: In their own words
Identifiers: LCCN 2016014825 (print) | LCCN 2016027722 (ebook) |
ISBN 9781572841895 (paperback) | ISBN 1572841893 (paperback) | ISBN
9781572847798 (ebook) | ISBN 1572847794 (ebook)
Subjects: LCSH: Ma, Yun, 1964---Quotations. | Business--Quotations, max-ims, etc. | BISAC: BUSINESS & ECONOMICS / Management. | BUSINESS &
ECONOMICS / Leadership. | BUSINESS & ECONOMICS / Entrepreneurship. |
BIOGRAPHY & AUTOBIOGRAPHY / Business.
Classification: LCC HC426.5.M327 N49 2016 (print) | LCC HC426.5.M327
(ebook) | DDC 650.092--dc23
LC record available at https://lccn.loc.gov/2016014825

B2 Books is an imprint of Agate Publishing. Agate books are available in bulk at discount prices. For more information, go to agatepublishing.com.

From Bob Song:
To my family, who has been super supportive

From Suk Lee:
*To all dreamers and entrepreneurs who are not afraid to
fail, to give birth to their passion and dreams*

Contents

Introduction

B ORN SEPTEMBER 10, 1964, JACK MA, or Ma Yun
(马云), is a Chinese entrepreneur and philanthropist. He is the founder and—until his retirement in September 2019—executive chairman of the Alibaba Group,
one of the world's most successful Internet-based companies. With an estimated net worth of USD$37 billion,
Ma is one of the wealthiest individuals on the planet.

His journey to the top is a true rags-to-riches story.
Before creating Alibaba, Ma was a humble English
teacher at Hangzhou Normal College. During a trip to
Seattle, Washington, in 1995, a friend introduced Ma
to the Internet. After searching for the words "beer"
and "China" and finding no results, Ma decided to start
an Internet company and bring the World Wide Web
to his country. He knew nothing about coding or computers, and few Chinese people understood what the
Internet was, let alone its potential in the marketplace,
prompting Ma to call himself "a blind man riding on the
back of a blind tiger." Despite these obstacles, Ma was
determined to start his business. He borrowed money
from relatives and set up an office with 17 partners in
his small apartment in Hangzhou. In the beginning, the
company made no money. It gave its services away for
free, expanded too quickly, and came close to folding.
After many false starts, Alibaba eventually built a platform for small- and medium-sized Chinese businesses

to connect to international buyers, and by its third year, the company was finally profitable. Ma's unique vision, positive spirit, and ceaseless determination have helped Alibaba become the most dominant e-commerce company in China today.

One of Ma's most famous mottos, "Never give up," reflects the attitude with which Ma has faced rejection throughout his life. He flunked his university exams twice, finally accepting a spot at what he calls "my city's worst university." Later on, Harvard's graduate school rejected him 10 times. When Kentucky Fried Chicken came to China, 24 people applied for jobs, and 23 people were accepted—he was the only person denied a position.

In 2015, *Forbes* named him one of the 22 most powerful people in the world, and in 2017 ranked him second on its World's Greatest Leaders list. Since Alibaba went public on September 19, 2014, and raised a record-breaking USD$25 billion IPO, Jack Ma and his company have been hot topics in the media world. He is the first mainland Chinese entrepreneur to appear on the cover of *Forbes* and has been in broadcasted conversation with leaders such as President Barack Obama.

Known for his humility, colorful candor, and exuberant personality, Jack Ma is a highly respected business icon in China. It's no wonder why: Alibaba has been instrumental in revolutionizing the country's commerce and entrepreneurship. It has established not only a first-class network for local and global business transactions but also a previously unheard-of method for trustworthy online payment (Alipay). Before Alibaba, China was a sea of millions of small- and medium-sized enterprises (SMEs) with no easy way to connect to customers or collect payment. For nearly two decades, Ma and his team have strived to create a positive, lucrative business environment for these operations, and Jack Ma has consistently eschewed and challenged the idea that the desires of Alibaba's shareholders should take precedence over the desires of its customers and employees. Because of Alibaba's focus on empowering SME owners, millions have been able to earn decent livings and support their families, a responsibility Ma has never seemed to take lightly as he's looked ever toward the future and Alibaba's goal of helping "2 billion consumers in the world shop online." Generous with his own employees, Ma has not been a typical executive chairman. He has been known to provide all-expenses-paid wedding ceremonies and over-the-top performances, like his costumed rendition of "Can You Feel the Love Tonight" at Alibaba's 10th anniversary celebration, and his impersonation of Michael Jackson when the company turned 18.

Ma's retirement from the chairmanship of Alibaba is in keeping with his spirit of generosity. Ma, who began his career as a teacher and says he often acted as a teacher at Alibaba, is leaving the company he started to return to the classroom. This time, he will not only be an educator but a philanthropist, using his vast fortune to fund educational improvement and reform. As an educator, Ma knows the importance of developing a talented staff—he frequently said "customer first, employees second, and shareholders third"—and after 20 years, he leaves behind a powerfully talented team at Alibaba. The current CEO, Daniel Zhang, has been named as his successor and will lead a staff of 86,833 with a mean age of 31.5 years. The world will be watching to see how

Alibaba fares without its visionary founder at the helm.

This book aims to provide readers around the world with a better understanding of Jack Ma through his own words, quoted from news articles, public statements, television interviews, and more. Although Ma speaks fluent English and is often interviewed on US media, we have also spent hundreds of hours mining content from Chinese media outlets, including coverage in China's biggest newspapers and television shows, as well as speeches from Alibaba's regular network operators meetings, which are multicity roadshows that allow Ma and his associates to teach local Alibaba users about services and business best practices. Quotations from these sources have been translated from the original Chinese, making Ma's valuable insights—on entrepreneurship, business values, e-commerce, charity, competition, and more—accessible for the first time to an English-speaking audience.

What emerges is a portrait of a man who has, in less than one generation, revolutionized the Chinese marketplace and the world of e-commerce at large—with absolutely no previous experience with business, technology, or frankly, success. This book is for anyone with a dream and ambition—or anyone who needs a little reminder to "never give up."

—*Suk Lee and Bob Song*

Part I

RUNNING A COMPANY

Business Principles

A COMMON MISSION, values, and goals are mandatory in any company or organization. Without these three things, you cannot succeed.

—Ningbo Network Operators Meeting, June 11, 2002

WHEN WE EMPLOY a person, we choose those who identify with our company values. No matter a person's individual talents, they must identify with our culture and ideals. From the first day of training, we talk about common values and team spirit. Together, this leads ordinary people to extraordinary achievement.

—"Jack Ma's Management," February 25, 2004

HOW CAN YOU sell Gucci or whatever branded bag for so much money? It is ridiculous. I understand the branded companies are not happy, but I also say that's your business model. You have to check your business model, too.

—*Forbes*, November 4, 2015

A SALESPERSON SHOULD not think about money but should consider how their product can help the customer's success and be useful to others. This will help their self-confidence and sales ability.

—Qingdao Network Operators Meeting, July 22, 2005

We adhere always to placing the customer first, employees second, and shareholders third.

—Alibaba's 10th anniversary celebration,
September 10, 2009

Our system does not rely on one or two people. If I leave and the company collapses, then it wasn't well constructed.

—APEC 5th e-Business Champions Grand Awards Ceremony, August 2, 2008

Two days ago, I had a dinner with my Singapore friends and they said, "Our government is encouraging us to have more babies because people are aging and there aren't enough kids." Every country, every nation, needs an incentive package to have more small- and medium-sized companies, to have more hopes. Every big company comes from a small business. Without this kind of hope, without this incentive to have more "babies," we're going to die. Why do I always feel excited? I have eight babies. In the past 15 years, I have built up eight companies. Seven of them are very healthy, and one of them—I sold it. When I look at my babies, Alibaba, Taobao, Alipay, and all the other companies—AliCloud, we just had a new baby two months ago—I always feel excited because you see the hope, and you know, "This baby is going to change me. This baby is going to change the world."

—APEC SME Global Summit, 2009

SAME AS EVERYBODY else, I hate KPI [key performance indicators]! It causes us to lose sight of our ideals and goals and exhausts us in several ways. It diminishes our working interest, innovation, and passion. So, we hate it, but we can't do without it! Really, the problem isn't KPI itself but rather the people who design and implement it.

WHAT IS KPI? KPI measures indicators in the realization of work targets. Without it, we lack specific indicators for evaluating work performance. It doesn't mean, however, that only through KPI can we complete good work. KPI is like going to the doctor where he takes your temperature, blood pressure, and blood for analysis. While it might prove you're not sick, it doesn't absolutely prove that you're healthy either.

—*Jack Ma's Management Diary*, 2009

Never deceive others, in business or in life. In 1995, I was deceived by four companies—four companies that are now closed. A company cannot go far by deceit.

—Shanghai Network Operators Meeting, July 2005

ALMOST ALL OF our vice presidents have stayed with us through the years. Still, it is important to have successors ready for staff replacement. The company should not be held hostage by key employees, nor those employees by the company. I myself was kidnapped by Alibaba several years ago. I let four key staff members take their holidays in shifts and study abroad for two to three years—meaning that I couldn't go anywhere.

Some say that Jack Ma "eliminates" his company's senior workers. But our successor system needs to be ready for those who have worked for decades and may be too tired, who have no friends except for their work colleagues. While it may appear that there is never a good time for them to take a leave of absence, they must. Once they are forced to do so, your younger workers will have their opportunity. We believe this in our hearts.

—Beijing Network Operators Meeting,
March 17, 2008

I THINK IN next 30 years, people [will]
only work four hours a day and maybe
four days a week.

—CNBC, June 21, 2017

CRITICISM FROM THE media, Internet
commentators, and investors isn't our
concern, only how users and business
people respond. If their response is
negative, we will be out of business.

—Digital China Forum, China Beijing International
High-Tech Industries Week, May 11, 2001

THE WORLD IS calling for a new commercial civilization. In the old commercial civilization, enterprises were self-centered and profit-centered instead of being society-centered. In the 21st century, enterprises should reconsider their relationship with society, the environment, humanity, and their clients. Today's enterprises must learn transparency, sharing, responsibility, and globalism to make for a better life in the 21st century.

—Alibaba's 10th anniversary celebration,
September 10, 2009

MANUFACTURING AND SERVICE industry
should be combined together. Manufacturing
will not be creating jobs because most of the
jobs on the manufacturing will be created
by AI and robots. Service industry is going
to be the area that creates a lot of jobs. Last
century we liked to be skilled, to [have]
standardization, and this century we need
personalization, customization.

> —World Trade Organization 2018 Public Forum,
> October 2, 2018

IT TAKES 30 percent of your time to lay the
foundation when building a house. A good
company, one with a stable and sizable income,
needs at least five years for success. . . . Alibaba
has not completed laying our foundation. We
run our business not because others are doing
it or because others wish us to do so. We do it
because we believe in what we do, when we
should do it, and how we should achieve it.

> —ChinaByte.com, July 2001

BEFORE I FIRST went to Japan, my general impression of Japanese companies and businessmen was positive. Not only did they attach importance to rules and etiquette but they did things diligently, dedicating attention to perfection.

I was surprised, however, once I visited Japan. Big enterprises there often delayed decisions and lost opportunities due to trivial things. While I respect people who seek perfection, it's fatal for an enterprise to delay decisive action when time and circumstance demand speed for success.

—*Nikkei Business,* May 2002

WE ASSESS EMPLOYEES on two standards: performance and team spirit.... Those with high performance but no team spirit are "wild dogs," and those with a good team spirit but low performance are "white rabbits." No dogs or rabbits as employees, please; they must excel at both.

—Xiamen Network Operators Meeting, September 2001

HIRE THE PERSON best suited to the job, not the most talented. This can be a very painful lesson. There's no point putting in a Boeing jet engine when you need to run a tractor.

—Dongguan Network Operators Meeting, March 2005

MONEY IS BETTER invested cultivating your company's talent through training and organization than in market promotion. Employees need to understand your company, your clients, and your competition. As the Chinese saying goes, "Know your enemies as you know yourself."

—*Nikkei Business,* May 2002

Alibaba and Other Ventures

FIRST WEEK, WE have seven employees. We buy and sell, ourselves. The second week, somebody started to sell on our website. We bought everything they sell. We had two rooms full of things we bought for no use, all garbage, for the first two weeks—in order to tell people that it works.

—**Economic Club of New York, June 9, 2015**

Smiling is very important to the culture at Alibaba. Our logo is a smile. When our employees and clients go home, I want them to be smiling. While I can't remember the face of every person who comes by the office, I identify if they are Alibaba staff by their smile.

—speech to Alibaba executives, June 16, 2006

WE ARE NOT an e-commerce company, although we have the largest e-commerce business in the world. We're not eBay. We do not buy and sell. We help people become an e-commerce company. We enable other companies to do e-commerce. This is the difference between us and Amazon. We believe every company should be an Amazon. Amazon is a traditional business that happens to have a website.

—Stanford Graduate School of Business,
September 24, 2015

OUR DREAM WAS to create the best company
in the world. Although Alibaba was started
by a Chinese person, we aspire to be a global
company of investors, employees, and clients,
not simply a Chinese company. Decisions are
driven by asking how do we become better,
not based on the value of our shares. Jack Ma
wishes to prove that an Internet company's
value comes from wisdom, strategy, courage,
and teamwork, not capital.

—*Fortune Life Program*, March 29, 2003

WE ARE NOT merely trying to shift buy/sell
transactions from offline to online, nor are
we changing conventional digital marketing
models to squeeze out a little additional profit.
We are working to create the fundamental
digital and physical infrastructure for
the future of commerce, which includes
marketplaces, payments, logistics, cloud
computing, big data and a host of other fields.

—letter to shareholders, October 13, 2016

I never want to make Alibaba as an empire, a business empire. No empire ends good. . . . We want to make Alibaba an ecosystem, like a forest.

—The New Economy Workshop, Government of Indonesia, March 21, 2018

THE DIFFERENCE BETWEEN us and Walmart, Walmart sell a lot of products. They have the data. They analyze that data because they want to sell more. We sell things because we want to have the data. Our sales is to improve our data experience.

—CNBC, September 2, 2016

OUR EMPLOYEES ARE trained to think the Alibaba way. No matter where they work in the world, they must come to Hangzhou for a month to learn both our mission and value concepts and company culture. Without this, they can't become Alibaba employees. We spend two hours telling trainees that their actions reflect their thoughts. Most of the time, salesmen think of how to get ¥5 from your pocket into theirs. Alibaba employees need to consider how they can keep that ¥5 in your pocket and change it into ¥50. Thinking this way makes us different.

—Dongguan Network Operators Meeting, March 2005

OUR CONCENTRATION ON e-commerce is persistent. Ten years ago, we concentrated on e-commerce, and we still concentrate on e-commerce. Ten years ago, we focused on medium and small companies, and we will still concentrate on medium and small companies. Because we concentrate on e-commerce and small and medium companies, we will operate for a long time.

—Alibaba's 10th anniversary celebration,
September 10, 2009

ONE OF THE secret sauces of Alibaba's success is that we have a lot of women . . . 47 percent of the employees of our company are women. We actually had 51 [percent], but we acquired some companies and they had more men, so the balance [went] down. Thirty-three percent of the management are women, and 24 percent of the senior management—very top level—are women. We have a woman CEO, CFO, CPO. . . . If you want to win in the 21st century, you have to make sure you are making other people powerful. Empower others. Make sure the other people are better than you are, and you will be successful. So I find that women think about the others more than they think about themselves.

—World Economic Forum, January 23, 2015

I'VE NEVER GOTTEN one cent from the government. I've never gotten one cent from Chinese banks. So I am very independent. I had a very strict talk with my team: Never, ever do business with the government. Love them. Don't marry them. So we never do projects for the government. If they come to us and say, "Jack, can you help us with this?" [I say] good—I will introduce friends to you who are interested in doing that. Or, if you want me to do it, I do it free for you, just next time, don't come to me again. Because of that, we keep a very good love-relationship with the government.

—*60 Minutes*, September 28, 2014

I USE MY computer and the Internet for two things: email and web browsing. Everything else is pretty much beyond me, even watching movies online. I ask our engineers for technology that serves people's needs. No matter how good that technology is, if people can't use it, it's worthless! Why is our website so popular with common business people? It's because I was the quality control—any programs written by our engineers had to be used by me. If I couldn't use it, it was trashed, because it meant that 80 percent of people as simple as I am wouldn't be able to use it either. My goal is that people can use it without even reading the manual.

—*Fortune Life Program*, March 29, 2003

RECENTLY OUR PERSONNEL changes have been frequent. I'm touched by the lack of complaint following all these changes. Things move fast in these times and in our current culture of information exchange. Alibaba's staff needs to welcome, embrace, and be ready for the challenge of all these changes.

—Alibaba's 5th anniversary celebration,
September 10, 2004

ALIBABA STANDS OUT not because our profits are bigger or our staff is more talented. It is because we emphasize foresight, strategy, system building, team training, and company culture from the beginning.

—Qingdao Network Operators Meeting, July 22, 2005

We want to make the company last for 102 years. And people are curious: Why 102 years? Because Alibaba was born in 1999—last year we had one year, this century we have 100 years, next century, one year. With 102, we'll cross three centuries.

—Economic Club of New York, June 9, 2015

He [Jerry Yang] said, "Call me." He said, "Jack, can you come and tonight we have our drink? For a final effort." And then I said, "Ok." So he took me to small, tiny Japanese restaurant and bought me big glass of sake. And we drank and [he] tried to convince me how wonderful Yahoo! is. And after drinking we said, "Ok, let's keep on talking." [That was] the most expensive sake I've ever had in my life. Now, I'm pretty sensitive about sake.

—Stanford Graduate School of Business,
September 24, 2015

[SINGLES DAY] IS not purely an online sales day. It is a day that the manufacturer, the business guys, communicate with the consumers. Consumers, it's the way they know the innovation, the new products, the new trends every year.... I think the American people, if they know that there will be products not only from China but also products from the Philippines, Kenya and Africa, Argentina, and all these nations, it will be unique.

—*Squawk on the Street*, November 11, 2014

[SINGLES DAY] IS a unique day. We want all the manufacturers, all the shop owners, to be thankful for the consumers. We want the consumers to have a wonderful day. It's special. Number wise, maybe there's not a big difference [in sales]. But for the event itself, the meaning of it, it's getting such great excitement in China.

—*Bloomberg Markets*, November 11, 2015

CLIENTS MUST BE willing to undergo training after they become Alibaba customers. We will establish an Ali College early next year to train employees and clients. We want our clients to grow together with Alibaba. They can come to our company for training every month, or we can go to different cities and gather clients together for training. Our courses include Alibaba product usage, management practices, small- and medium-enterprise development, etc. This is what we run at Alibaba College.

—Harvard–Tsinghua Senior Executive Program,
December 2003

THE SPEED WITH which our Taobao website took off surprised the US media completely— they thought eBay was invincible! They weren't willing to believe a pure Chinese website could compete with major players such as eBay, Yahoo!, and others. But Taobao's user data forced US analysts to look at us with new eyes. Only then did they realize that C2C competition within China was far fiercer than anything they had imagined.

—*Reuters*, September 27, 2004

WHILE ALIPAY NOW seems very successful, we were forced to come up with the idea for it. Back then, transactions on Taobao were difficult because we hadn't solved the problem of secure payment. Our big domestic banks didn't want to get involved, so we turned to foreign ones such as Citigroup and HSBC.

At a meeting that year, one executive advised, "How do you innovate and make decisions for your future? That's your mission." That's when we came up with Alipay. We do it cleanly and transparently, reporting to the relevant departments every quarter.

—*Zheshang Online*, March 31, 2011

CHINA TODAY, BECAUSE of the pollution—of the air, of the food, of the water—we're going to have a lot of health problems. We can use our technology, our know-how to solve the problem. That's why we have to invest money today—to get ready for 10 years from now, when China has problems.

—*Bloomberg Markets*, November 11, 2015

LOOK AT THE world today. Especially China. The rich people aren't happy. The poor people aren't happy. The government officers are not happy. . . . I want people in China to enjoy the happiness of digital products—the movies, the theaters, the TV programs—all the digital content that makes the young people enjoy their lives, to be optimistic about the future.

—*Bloomberg Markets*, November 11, 2015

IN THE FUTURE, technology has to be fun. Alibaba has the 2H strategy for our future: happiness and health. If the advent of technology cannot make people happier and healthier, there is no point doing it.

—*South China Morning Post*, April 21, 2016

WE ALL KNEW that no one could stay with the company for 102 years. A sustainable Alibaba would have to be built on sound governance, culture-centric philosophy, and consistency in developing talent. No company can rely solely on its founders. Of all people, I should know that. Because of physical limits on one's ability and energy, no one can shoulder the responsibilities of chairman and CEO forever.

—letter to customers, employees, and shareholders,
September 9, 2018

Competition

Competition is a must. It is a painful process that forces your company to grow. Choose the best to compete with, but never take it personally.

—Shanghai Network Operators Meeting, July 2005

IF EVERYTHING COULD be won by money, then banks would control all the biggest companies. Running your business well against strong competition should provide a level of contentment that allows employees, shareholders, partners, and clients to all sleep well. In this way, the enterprise will become better and better.

—Beijing Network Operators Meeting, March 17, 2008

ALIBABA IS LIKE a crocodile in the Yangtze River. To fight with a shark in the sea is to lose. However, if we fight in the Yangtze River, we surely will not be defeated. eBay came to China to do battle in our native country where we have home-field advantage. Here it is OK for us to eat a bowl of noodles for ¥3 and rather stupid to spend ¥300 for the same. eBay invests ¥70 billion in the Chinese market to our mere ¥100 million. But what can they do better than us?

—CNBC, October 23, 2004

IT'S NOT ABOUT beating a competitor to "win," because there'll always be another competitor. Consider it more like an ecosystem of land, water, and biodiversity with all kinds of competing interests. This competition hones you and helps you to grow.... In such an ecosystem, the lion kills the antelope not because he hates antelope but because he needs to eat. You defeat your competitor not because of how powerful you are but because those who aren't willing to improve themselves remain stuck in the past and lose the future. If their technology is inferior, they must improve it. If their staff's quality is inferior, it must be made better. Think ecologically and look for a "win-win" with opponents. We're all in this together. Without lions, antelopes can't live to their fullest.

—Hangzhou 8th E-Businessmen's Convention,
September 10, 2011

Don't fight
your rivals but
embrace them
and analyze their
core concepts.
No rival can kill
you—only you can
kill yourself.

—Shanghai Network Operators Meeting, July 2005

Do I like competition? Yes. Competition allows you to improve yourself, be better, and in the process, make your rivals angry. An angry fighter is not a good fighter.

—Beijing Network Operators Meeting,
March 17, 2008

IT'S UNFORTUNATE THAT Alibaba has no competitor. We get tired searching for competitors everywhere. Taobao, however, is lucky enough to have eBay as a great competitor. If you have to box with Mike Tyson, you might think yourself unlucky. But this type of world-class competitor is good. Think of your good fortune getting to play basketball against Michael Jordan. Taobao can learn a lot from a competitor such as eBay.

—*Beijing Morning Post*, October 21, 2004

WHEN CONFRONTING COMPETITION, be mindful of four things. The first one is that which you can't see. The second is that which you look down on. Third is that which you can't understand, and finally, the fourth one, after trying all methods, is that which you can't follow up on.

—Qingdao Network Operators Meeting, July 22, 2005

THE QUESTION YOU must ask is: "If we fund a competitive price war with our own savings (not our investors' money) will we have full support?" The need in most companies is not so much capital and technology as it is critical thinking. Always ask who are you fighting for, why you are fighting, and how you'll fight. Then prepare for the worst. We must protect both the consumer's rights and the manufacturer's interests to the max. This is the key principle to success. If a price war for your "honor" uses investors' money to hold manufacturers hostage and deceive consumers, the cost is too high.

—internal speech to Alibaba employees,
August 27, 2012

Some will say
they want to beat
Taobao or defeat
Alibaba. It sounds
great, but really,
only our own
stubbornness can
defeat us.

—Hangzhou 8th E-Businessmen's Convention,
September 10, 2011

IF YOU ONLY have a small- to medium-sized Internet business, don't compete with NetEase, Sina, Sohu, and Alibaba on scale or size. Compete only on what you can do in the professional market that they can't.

—NetEase.com, February 17, 2004

WE RANK FIRST in some of our industries and second in others. Some of our ventures fail to make money and die. Ranking second while still spending little, making good money, and being influential is fine. Indeed, some of our e-commerce is specifically targeted at this second position. However, none of our e-commerce is targeted for third place. Be either first or second, never third. If after two years of being third we cannot pass into second, then it is time to close that venture.

—speech to welcome China Yahoo! team to Alibaba, September 23, 2005

IF OUR COMPETITOR is loaded with bullets, we'll try to get him to shoot them into a wall. With the right strategy, competition should be an amusement, a game—not a source of pain. Conceiving the strategy of this game unites your employees and you. Remember, the first to lose their temper, loses the game.

—Shanghai Network Operators Meeting, July 2005

WE ARE NOT competing with Amazon. . . . We have a pretty different model. They buy and sell. Alibaba is a platform. . . . We believe every company can be an Amazon. We think if Amazon is a great apple, Alibaba is the apple tree. We want to enable every company to be an e-commerce company. We want a lot of people to be as successful as Amazon.

—*Bloomberg Markets*, November 11, 2015

It's difficult for an elephant to step on all the ants because the ants won't allow it. They'll run here and there. And the elephant may break a leg trying to step on them all.

—*Beijing Morning Post*, October 21, 2004

CAN ALIBABA BE copied? Our methods, maybe, but not our team and the wisdom gained from our mistakes. Nor can you copy my thoughts, our clients' trust, or the opportunities they've presented us. This does not mean that another company won't ever surpass us. We may see 100, 200, or even 1,000 e-commerce websites created. In the Chinese e-commerce market, I hope many more websites will innovate and exploit opportunities. If Alibaba's own site remains a work in progress, there'll be little need to copy us five years from now.

—Shenzhen Network Operators Meeting,
March 5, 2008

WHEN WE COMPETED with eBay ... there are
a lot of things we can learn from the other
guys, from other companies. But today, the
things we are doing, there's nothing we can
learn from.

—Bloomberg, September 14, 2017

YOUR COMPANY'S CORE competitiveness is
your team and you. Others may copy your
model, but not your constant persistence
and passion. Behind the best innovation,
of course, there must be a strong support
system, talent, and execution. Without this,
innovation is merely a story without value.

—Win in China, August 2007

Money, Investment, and Value

ORIGINALLY, ALIBABA HAD a single board of directors to answer to our investors. Now we're divided into five companies, each one with its own board, to eliminate the risk of one investor controlling everything. While I respect shareholders and occasionally even listen to them, I act on my own ideas. I hear from my staff too, but still do what I think is right. But for customers, I'm all ears and try to follow their advice as much as possible. Customers first, employees second, shareholders third—this order doesn't change because of an IPO and the stock market.

—*Caijing Magazine*, August 1, 2007

[Investors] love me, they hate me, but I love them.

—*Bloomberg Markets*, November 11, 2015

FOR SUCCESSFUL BUSINESS leaders, if their goal is to be rich, they can become very rich. But then what's the point of having all that money? When you have 100 million U.S. dollars, I think that's more than enough for you and your children. Once your net worth exceeds a certain point, that's not your money anymore. It is society's money. It is the money society has given to you, and you should take responsibility to allocate the money in a good way. I started thinking about this issue just two, three years ago. One day I suddenly woke up and wondered, "What's next?"

—Nature.org, December 2009

YOU AMERICANS LOVE to spend tomorrow's money. And other people's money, maybe. We Chinese love to save money. We are probably the largest safe deposit in the whole world. 'Cause we've been poor for so many years. When we made money, we put it in the banks, because someday we know that disaster is coming, and we can spend the money [then]. So when the economy is bad, we still have the money to spend. You guys probably don't.

—2015 Clinton Global Initiative Annual Meeting, September 29, 2015

IN 1999, AT a time when Internet companies were lucky to last eight months, we said our plan was to run our business for 80 years. This target of 80 years weeded out speculators interested only in chasing and cashing in on an IPO.

—Dongguan Network Operators Meeting, March 2005

IN 1999, I told shareholders on the first day of financing that Alibaba's investors were our uncles. Clients are our parents. Since I get along so well with my "uncles," shareholders' meetings now run shorter than ever and are fun.

—China National Computer Congress, October 12, 2010

IF YOUR CEO serves 10,000 clients, then your team should serve 100,000 clients. These 100,000 clients should serve 1 million clients. You create the most value when your clients can help other clients.

—Hangzhou Network Operators Meeting, September 15, 2007

I KNOW LOTS of smart people, but Masayoshi Son [CEO of SoftBank] is unique. He may look dull and speak weird English but he has great wisdom even as he appears a little slow-witted. More than 700 companies apply annually for investment from SoftBank. They invest in about 10 percent of them, and Masayoshi Son negotiated directly only with one: us. His words to me: "I invest in you because of your unique leadership. Keep it up!"

—preface to *Fly Higher*, 2006

Finding the right investment companies is like choosing a marriage partner. We need to be hand in hand through tough times. Today, everything may be fine, but tomorrow, if our luck turns, I'll need your support.

—Xiamen Network Operators Meeting, September 2001

AT A STAFF meeting in February I said we needed to prepare for when winter came. It was not a time to take things for granted. When speculation tripled our share price following our [Hong Kong IPO] listing, I was mindful of dark clouds and thunder gathering even amidst the cheers and applause. Passion and fever that come quickly can fade with the same amazing speed. I wasn't willing to lose sight and lack reason concerning the sharp rise in share price.

During the listing ceremony, I said that we would go on as always. We would not change our mission. Forget share-price fluctuations and remember clients come first. We have a long-term promise to our clients, society, shareholders, and their families. When these promises are fulfilled, then our share price will naturally reflect the value created by the company.

—"The Winter Mission," email to Alibaba employees, July 23, 2008

FOR THE ALIBABA Group, our IPO in Hong Kong today is only a beginning. We're fueling up in a gas station for a long trip ahead.

—**press conference for Hong Kong Stock Exchange IPO listing, November 6, 2007**

EQUITY SHOULD BE dispersed. Wisdom, not financing, should influence company management and employee teamwork. Our more than 1,000 employees are our biggest shareholder, with Masayoshi Son's SoftBank next. As market value grows, this management and employee shareholder ratio can be adjusted.

—**NetEase.com, February 17, 2004**

BUT WHEN YOU have $1 billion, remember:
That is not your money. That is the people's
expectation of you. People put their hope on
you, because people believe you can manage
this money, resources, better than the others.
If you think this is your money, you will be in
trouble.

—Stanford Graduate School of Business,
September 24, 2015

WHY DID WE create Alibaba? Our goal is to
make our clients millionaires. We put clients
first. Only when they succeed can Alibaba
then succeed. Our profitability comes only
after our clients become millionaires and
multimillionaires.

—Alibaba's 5th anniversary celebration,
September 10, 2004

MANY OF OUR employees wonder why
they aren't out in front, considering
our "people first" policy. We're not being
hypocritical. When we gather as a group to
solve Alibaba members' problems, we can't
have distractions of "employees first" or
"shareholders first" taking focus away from
resolving website issues. Whenever I meet
with clients, I want to hear that they make
money with Alibaba. My biggest fear is
hearing that they're not profitable. So, when
I meet with shareholders, I can argue what
our priorities must be even if they don't feel
good about it.

—Shenzhen Network Operators Meeting,
November 2005

Never think about financing when creating a business. You will never create a good company that way. Don't chase after investors (they'll only run away faster) but know that, as a successful small- to medium-sized company, investors will come to you. Money will then be a happy surprise.

—NetEase.com, February 17, 2004

WHEN WE LAUNCHED Taobao two years ago, we offered it free. Alibaba also provided three years of free service. Almost all of our services are launched free for the first year or two. The main reason is to understand our clients' needs during this period. Then we make adjustments accordingly. But if you find then that you can't generate any traffic even as a free service, it's hopeless. You may not have any value. We gained lots of valuable experience during our free period, so that today, things are very good. We now have USD$1 billion and can provide even more free service.

—*Fortune Life Program*, March 2003

I'M HUMBLE BECAUSE I think many years ago people said, "Well, Alibaba's a terrible company." And I knew we were not that terrible. We were pretty good. We were better than people thought. But today, when people have a high expectation of us, I start to worry and become nervous, because we are not that good yet. We are a company that is only 15 years old. We are running an Internet business in China. The average age of the young people [here in China] is only 28 years old. So it's a young company, young industry, and it's not easy. When people have a high expectation of us, I want to tell myself and tell our team, "Be ourself. Do whatever we believe is right." I don't dare to watch the stock price . . . when people think you are good, you have to be sure that you're really that good. When people think you're bad, you have to be clear whether [or not] you are really that bad.

—*Squawk on the Street*, November 11, 2014

Media and Marketing

"ALIBABA" IS EASY to pronounce in almost all the languages of the world. This makes it easy for all potential customers to accept and use our website name.

—World Economic Forum, January 23, 2015

ADVERTISING CAN HELP in recognition, but branding is built by public response. It's a cultural value that can never be hammered home by advertising alone. Advertising increases costs and can reach a point where your client can't afford it. You must sustain a quality team and company culture, otherwise advertising will only bring added costs, not benefits.

—Alibaba blog, March 19, 2012

COMMUNICATION PROBLEMS CAN exist despite your best planning. In May, we held an important introductory "Expand Your Wealth" event at no charge. Everyone then expected future events would be free, too, but we found it necessary to have an entry fee. Although our competitors routinely charged for the same thing, we were criticized for this. We had no one to blame but ourselves for not having better PR and getting word out. In a new product launch for clients, there are four indispensible steps: convince them logically, motivate them emotionally, tempt them monetarily, and be fair and just to them.

—**remarks to Alibaba executives, June 16, 2006**

IN 1995, I explained incessantly that the Internet existed, but not many people were willing to trust it. They couldn't see how this Internet could be a great contribution to the lives of people.

I felt then that the Internet would impact all aspects of human life. But when Jack Ma said this, nobody would believe it. So instead, I started to say that Bill Gates was claiming the Internet would change the way people live. The media picked up on this. But actually, it is what I was saying then. In 1995, even Bill Gates wasn't a believer in the Internet. Later, I apologized to Bill Gates for this a number of times when I met him.

—Henen Youth Entrepreneurship Forum,
October 25, 2008

SIX YEARS AGO, our PR guy told me I had to start doing interviews. I resisted, unwilling to meet with any media. I feel I'm ugly enough that people remember me from first sight. If I walk down the street, everyone will know me. I didn't want this. However, after hounding me for three days, our PR guy said, "Jack Ma. This name doesn't just belong to you, it belongs to Alibaba." After that, I started to do interviews. From then until now, the media links Alibaba completely with Jack Ma. But please don't trust the media too much: The person they build up with praise one day can be brought down with attacks the next. Being "ordinary" is a glamour all its own.

—Qingdao Network Operators Meeting, July 22, 2005

ALIBABA HAS A very good PR team, very capable. Our only secret is to always tell the truth. No matter wherever or whenever, say what you're thinking. Don't say things that the media loves to hear or deceive them in order to cater to them. Tell a lie now, and you'll be forced to keep it going even as you forget parts of it. This will only cause lots of pain. People like honesty. Not many people, however, will tell the truth at any time. Do so and you'll differ from others.

—Chinabyte.com, July 2001

OUR PROMOTIONAL BUDGET this past year was zero even as our name has grown greatly. This "miraculous" rise in branding has even caught the attention of the Harvard Business School. But there's no miracle. From 1995 through 1999, we had five years of hardship, but now, Alibaba will do even better next year. We learn not only from our own mistakes but from those made by other Chinese Internet companies, too.

—TrustPass press conference, March 10, 2002

August 1999 was the first time we met with the media. Somehow, *Businessweek* in the US found out about Alibaba. At first, we refused their interview request. Later, we accepted via the Ministry of Foreign Affairs and the Foreign Affairs Office in Zhejiang Province. At the time, we didn't even have an office telephone or fax machine. We did have a US address, however, so that we wouldn't be thought of solely as a local Chinese company and regarded globally as a third-class enterprise. For the interview, when we took the reporter to the residential area where we were based, they regarded us with suspicion. When we opened the door, we had 20 to 30 people crammed inside the four-bedroom flat. The interviewer thought Alibaba, with our big reputation and thousands of members, should have already been a very big company. In the end, that article was never published.

—Ningbo Network Operators Meeting, June 11, 2002

A LOCAL HANGZHOU newspaper implied in print that our private-enterprise Internet company lacked any real standing. In order to prove differently, we introduced our company with English PR materials sent from the US by courier. We printed out pages from our US website in color to show we were an international Internet presence. This was a difficult start. Later we realized that rabbits naturally eat the grass by their own burrows first, and we should have made friends locally from the beginning.

All this helps in credibility. I'm lucky now in that even if I were to leave this company, I could still finance USD$30 million with one telephone call. That's credibility. I have a large number of entrepreneurial students, and their trust is based on my credibility. Of course, you must use this credibility well and do what you say. We've walked the walk by relying on this belief.

—CCTV Innovation Forum, December 8, 2005

FOR US, THE Internet is a tool. Why is it so powerful? I'm a big fan of martial arts fiction. No matter how great a person's swordplay, however, someone with a gun can still kill them because it's a more powerful weapon. Compared with word of mouth from your relatives and friends or publicity from magazines, newspapers, and conventional media, the Internet will certainly become more powerful. If you miss this opportunity, you'll be out of luck. Never look down upon new and emerging tools. Use this new tool well and your enterprise will be better. Use it poorly, or not at all, and you'll suffer.

—Wenzhou Network Operators Meeting,
November 19, 2001

Part II

EYE ON THE FUTURE

Entrepre-neurship and Innovation

WE NEVER PROMISE that as Alibaba employees you'll enjoy nonstop promotions and share in lots of wealth. We do promise, however, that you'll have a steady share of our difficulties, depression, and pain.

If you've been with us less than a year, please spare us Alibaba strategy reports and development plans. Better you should open an exit door on your way out than your mouth. However, if you've been here at least three years, I'm all ears, happy to hear your suggestions for our growth, and grateful for your intention to make us better.

Remember, Alibaba doesn't pay you for your own personal development but for helping our customers in their growth. We develop ourselves through our customers.

—internal email to employees, August 27, 2011

ONE WORD: SURVIVAL. Small and medium enterprises need unique survival methods. Opportunity exists in danger. A big crisis may take down larger companies, allowing small- to medium-sized businesses to emerge. Think through three questions: 1) What do you want to do? 2) What should you do? 3) How long do you do it for?

What do you want to do? You must have an ideal and a dream you're willing to give up your house for. What should you do? It's critical that you think about this from the very beginning. Easy to say, difficult to do. How long do you do it for? No matter the industry, count on at least 30 chances in your first five years. Insist on this principle no matter outside temptations and pressure.

—Beijing Network Operators Meeting, March 17, 2008

[For] most people, seeing is believing. But real entrepreneurs and leaders, we believe, then we see. We believe the future, then we will see the future.

—Gateway '17, September 25, 2017

No matter what, you must have a dream. This is the best working capital to start with. Second, keep at it. There may be smarter people and more industrious people, but why did we succeed and make money when others didn't? We kept at it. Others didn't see a future for the Internet or the value in search engines, e-commerce, or a B2B network. While others went bankrupt, we kept at it. . . . Not thinking they'd find another job anyway, our employees stayed on and muddled through until we all became much better.

—Hangzhou Network Operators Meeting,
September 15, 2007

My grandmother has only one shirt in her wardrobe. My mother has three; my daughter's generation, fifty. And 48 percent of them, eh, she never wears them. This is called domestic consumption. And we have to build up this kind of behavior and make people start to spend money. And this is something the government is not good at. We [entrepreneurs] know how to make this thing happen.

—Stanford Graduate School of Business,
September 24, 2015

It's not about the money, it's about the dreams. It's not only about the technology that will change the world. It's about the dreams you believe that change the world.

—Economic Club of New York, June 9, 2015

UNDERSTAND WHO YOU are, the reasons for
your success. As to our present situation,
we first need to thank the emergence of the
Internet. Without the Internet, we could not
possibly have such revolutionary business
ideas. Second, we need to show gratitude
for the high-speed development of China's
economy. For this, I thank my team. Having
put up with me for five years, they still
believe in and follow me. But it's not Jack
Ma who's very capable and smart—it's my
employees.

—Shenzhen Network Operators Meeting,
March 5, 2008

I CALL ALIBABA "1,001 mistakes." We
expanded too fast, and then in the dot-com
bubble, we had to have layoffs. By 2002,
we had only enough cash to survive for 18
months. We had a lot of free members using
our site, and we didn't know how we'd make
money. So we developed a product for China
exporters to meet U.S. buyers online. This
model saved us. By the end of 2002, we made
$1 in profits. Each year we improved. Today,
Alibaba is very profitable.

—*Inc.*, January 1, 2008

I'm not a salesman, I'm an evangelist. And I want to say that evangelists believe in the future. Engineers believe in technology. And I believe technology is for the future.

—Alibaba Investor Day, June 8, 2017

There are so many opportunities in the world, in this world, because there are so many complaints. If you can solve the complaint, one of the complaints, that's the opportunity.

—Tel Aviv University, May 3, 2018

I N 1995, I started my business with nothing. Capital consisted of collective willpower and teamwork. Many entrepreneurs say without money they can't start anything. This is wrong. Entrepreneurs should be guided by responsibility and teamwork, not money. True entrepreneurs don't think of money first but only about their dream to start a company. Money is the final element.

—Alibaba's 5th E-Business Champions Grand Awards Ceremony, August 2, 2008

Roughly speaking, smaller businesses rely on their operation, medium ones on their management, and big companies on their teamwork. For this team, there are three key things to have: a far-reaching vision, a broad mind, and an ability to accomplish big things. As Hu Xueyan once said, "The more difficult it is to start a business, the better the opportunity down the road as long as you can see that far ahead."

—Wenzhou Network Operators Meeting,
November 19, 2001

A company's identity is somewhat similar to a zoo's. Just as a zoo is enhanced by having a wide variety of animals, so too does a company benefit from a talented staff representing all walks of life. This can only aid in innovation.

—"Lakeside Talk," June 24, 2007

I NEVER SAY that I'm a winner. Rather than claim success, I prefer to state that I conquer many difficulties. Every day, I face challenges and encounter problems that must be overcome. This is my main achievement. From day one, all entrepreneurs know that their day is about dealing with difficulty and failure rather than defined by "success."

My most difficult time hasn't come yet, but it surely will. Nearly a decade of entrepreneurial experience tells me these difficult times can't be evaded or shouldered by others—the entrepreneur must be able to face failure and never give up.

—CCTV website, 2004

BAD IDEAS ARE OK. We're not afraid of bad ideas as much as having no ideas. Never be afraid of taking quick action to solve current and future problems. We review not only our own website but also that of other businesses and even our competitors to see what good ideas can be put into practice immediately.

—ICBU Mobilization Meeting, June 13, 2007

BE READY FOR the difficulty and the daily grind. Nobody succeeds right from the start. I made lots of mistakes and gained lots of experience early on. For an entrepreneur, this is good. Don't just think about how much money you can make. If you do, you'll set yourself up for some painful lessons, especially for Internet start-ups. Today there may be many successful network operators, but none made money at all in their first three years.

—Hangzhou Network Operators Meeting, June 13, 2004

You MUST BE ready to bear the pressure, criticism, and loneliness that come with being an innovator. At first we were called cheaters, then crazy, and now complete lunatics. No matter what other people say, however, we believe in our company and ourselves. I don't care how others look at us but rather how we look at the world. Knowing how to move forward to meet your dream is the way of the entrepreneur.

—CCTV Innovation Forum, December 8, 2005

As AN EXTREME example, I would often disagree with what 90 percent of my staff agreed on at a company meeting. I think the best situation is when half of you agree and half disagree and you hash it out. Your competitors are also discussing these things, so it's a good test in finding your own way.

—Qingdao Network Operators Meeting, July 22, 2005

No MATTER WHAT country, small and medium enterprises are the main source of innovation.

Once your enterprise becomes big, innovation concerns itself with the scale of the operation. At this point, my thought is that you always need to look outside your company for further innovation.

—Boao Forum for Asia, April 14, 2008

It's not the regulators' regulations that solved the problems. It's innovation that solved the problems.

—World Trade Organization 2018 Public Forum,
October 2, 2018

WELL, TRUST THE young people, trust this generation's innovation. They're making things, changing innovation every day. And all the consumers are the same. They want new things. They want cheap things. They want good things. They want unique things. If we can create these kinds of things for consumers, they will come.

—*Squawk on the Street,* November 11, 2014

The Internet, E-Commerce, and Global Trading

So ONE DAY, later in 1996, China was connected to the Internet.... I invited 10 media friends to my apartment. I wanted to tell them, "I'm not telling a lie, there is a network called Internet." We waited three hours and a half to download the first picture. And people said, "Is that thing going to work?" And I said, "Yeah, it'll work, but not today. In 10 years, it'll work." But at least it proved I was not telling a lie.

—Economic Club of New York, June 9, 2015

E-commerce in the US is a dessert. It's complementary to the main business. But in China, it becomes the main course.

—Economic Club of New York, June 9, 2015

FROM THE AMERICAN point of view, Amazon probably is the only business model for e-commerce, but no, we are different. . . . We show great respect for eBay and Amazon, but I think the opportunity and the strategy for us is helping small business in America go to China, sell their products in China. . . . China has been focused on exporting for the past 20 years, and I think in the next 10 to 20 years China should be focusing on importing. China should learn to buy, China should spend the money, China should buy a lot of its things globally. And I think that American small business [selling] American-branded products should use the Internet and go to China.

—**Economic Club of New York, June 9, 2015**

TRUMP VERY MUCH cares about the small- and medium-sized company exporting. My thinking is that if we prove that we can achieve something by helping American small businesses export to China and helping small businesses sell things to Asia and to other countries, he will change.

—*South China Morning Post*, June 23, 2017

THE U.S. HAS been a consistent defender of free and open markets, but this time [with Trump's trade tariffs against China] it is resorting to protectionism that will not improve American competitiveness. Any country seeking to increase exports would do better to focus on developing good products and channels to access foreign markets rather than putting up trade barriers.

—*Wall Street Journal*, April 11, 2018

Long term, China will have a new model. China must open its market.

—Alibaba Investor Day, September 18, 2018

I THINK A healthy and positive China-US relationship is so critical, especially this century. Number one, number two economy in the world, if they're working together, they can solve a lot of problems: poverty, disease, environment. But if they don't work [together], it's going to be disaster.

—CNN, November 14, 2016

GLOBALIZATION MEANS CARING about what's happening in the entire world. You have to have a global horizon. Even the problems in a small African country can affect you. You need to have that mind-set to succeed.

—South China Morning Post China Conference, December 2, 2016

FIRST, WHEN US and international enterprises enter China, their biggest problem is dealing with Chinese bureaucracy. But rather than preoccupy themselves with *guanxi*, they need to create value for the Chinese market. Success in America doesn't guarantee the same in China, and it is crucial for these companies to adapt Chinese characteristics.

Second, leadership plays a very important role. In China, these international companies' leaders must have foresight in their pioneering efforts here rather than managing simply to safeguard established US and European brands.

Third, the Chinese economy is an entrepreneurial economy. Everyone is full of vitality and everything is possible. It's like Silicon Valley in the late 90s, with entrepreneurial passion and prosperity everywhere.

—Forbes Global CEO Conference, September 21, 2004

THEY SAY THESE are the three *s*'s for commercial success: be strong, scalable, and sustainable. However, I think these three points cannot be achieved in the current Internet business model. Only a stupid businessman tells others how he plans to make money in a complicated and competitive situation.

—89th Canton Fair, April 13–26, 2001

INVARIABLY, MISTAKES ARE made when starting a business. The important comments come from your clients—if users find your service useful, then it is. If they say it's useless, no matter what you say about it, it is. In e-commerce, electronics are the tool, commerce the goal. Investors can talk your product up to the high heavens, but if users regard your product without value or utility, you'll be crashing to earth in no time. As I say to my staff, "Don't tell me how to make money. Just tell me how to provide value to our clients."

—Xiamen Network Operators Meeting,
September 2001

Trade is a freedom. Trade is a human right. Trade should not be used as a tool against other nations.

—in conversation with President Barack Obama,
APEC CEO Summit, November 18, 2015

When trade stops, war starts.

—Fortune Global Forum, December 5, 2017

THE WORLD IS getting so small. Young people are mobile, they want to travel around the world. When you travel around the world, you exchange culture, you want to make friends, you want to exchange things. It's impossible and this is why we want to put a proposal [for] eWTP [Electronic World Trade Platform] [in the 2016 G20 agenda]. The world has changed. Let's [use] a new way to do trade. Let's think about in the past . . . hundreds of years, trade is organized or controlled by government. Let's think about private sectors. Let's think about how can business move trade.

—CNBC, September 2, 2016

THE FIRST TECHNOLOGY revolution had the business model called a factory. The second technology revolution, there was a business model called "company." . . . What will be the best business model for this century? We think [it] is something called like a platformed business. . . . Fifteen years ago we start to move our company from a normal . . . website to a platform.

—Alibaba Investor Day, June 8, 2017

SOME MANAGEMENT EXPERTS claim it's hard to survive as a middleman. Therefore, I'm often asked if we will expand into selling or move to manufacturing to ensure future development. When the phone was invented, people said the post office was done for. However, the post office lives on. It's very difficult for one industry to completely replace another. E-commerce won't displace middlemen, but will develop with a new type of middleman. There are no "bad" industries, only bad businesses. This new go-between will rely more and more on technology skills. They will understand the changes that are needed. As such, they will surely be needed in the future, even a hundred years from now.

—*First Financial Daily*, January 26, 2006

FOUR YEARS AGO, when we grow so fast, we got a lot of complaints about traditional retail. They say, "Hey, e-commerce take away all of our jobs, all of our business." So we ask ourselves, "Are we wanting to serve our customers, or are we wanting to kill all the retail, the traditional retail?" We think we should [be] working together. We believe online, off-line should [be] working together. With the data, with the customer experience, we think retail, the traditional retail, has huge potential if we do it properly, if we work together.

—*Squawk Box*, December 5, 2017

E-COMMERCE IS HOT now. Many companies want to join in this Internet bazaar but have nowhere to turn for a successful example. They are reluctant to continue without proof it can help them profit. So, when asked to show them a successful project, I point to Alibaba. By gathering a large group of "shrimps," small- to medium-sized enterprises, we can attract whales to come feed on them. Small and medium enterprises then become the solution for successful e-commerce.

—**TrustPass press conference, March 10, 2002**

IT'S NOT WHITE and black. If you just say, "Take that down," [to counterfeiters] it is unfair to that guy [the seller]. We have to also protect these guys, not only the branded businesses. You have to care about all the people, their rights.

—***Forbes*, November 4, 2015**

ASIANS IN BUSINESS believe it is better to be the head of a dog than the tail of a lion. Everybody wants to be their own boss and the Internet favors individuality even further. That is, the Internet user is self-centered, a brick on the Great Wall marked "I was here." When the Internet was introduced, there was already an overload of information. My goal was to do one thing: provide an "essence" of needed information that small- and medium-sized Asian companies would use all the time. The American model, based on being a big company, could spend a million dollars on software, but not many Chinese companies can afford that or even use such software. Chinese B2B emphasizes face-to-face communication between business people.

—89th Canton Fair, April 13–26, 2001

IN THE COMING decade, the Internet
will make the long-awaited transition
from a marketing channel into a virtual
infrastructure that will allow smaller
companies, which are really the major
engines of innovation, to compete effectively
with major corporations.

The ability to identify or create new
business opportunities around the world
will be limitless. For example, a business
that starts in China or India will have ability
to compete with one in Indiana. More
importantly, the Indiana business that has
the right attitude and global outlook will
not only be able to compete with India and
China, but also with bigger American and
European corporations.

—*New York Times*, October 26, 2009

Today we see "Made in China," "Made in America," "Made in Switzerland," and "Made in Geneva." 2030, we'll see "Made in Internet."

—World Trade Organization 2018 Public Forum,
October 2, 2018

AFTER LOTS OF research, we found that the number one thing for e-commerce is trust and credibility. Business people are most concerned with this. Last year, both our national and international media stated that while many people visited the Alibaba website, there was a lack of trust because it was based in China with mostly Chinese business users. They claimed that European websites, although small, were like an intimate Internet exhibition hall. Our large website was more like an Internet bazaar. Later, we found ways to establish a more credible system and plan to expand on this.

—TrustPass press conference, March 10, 2002

WHEN I COME to the SMEs [small- and medium-sized businesses], I always feel excited. Because when I join the SME conference I see from your eyes the dreams, the passion, the hope. When I join the Fortune 500 conference, I see the numbers, I see the revenues, I see the KPIs, I see the bloody competition.

—**APEC SME Global Summit, 2009**

Environmentalism and Philanthropy

THE CHINESE PEOPLE really care about environmental protection in China. That will be their greatest contribution to the world. For me, I have the luxury to think about doing more for Africa. But how many people are like Jack Ma? How many Chinese people have the resources, the opportunity to develop a bigger world view, and have the luxury to see the outside world? Obligation to the world is good, but I think the Chinese people will say they have an obligation to take more action to take care of their own environment. If you don't or can't care for yourself, I don't think you can care for others.

—Nature.org, December 2009

Instead of simply donating money, Taobao can contribute more by providing good career prospects for 10 million people. If these people have no opportunity or income, a stable society is simply an illusion.

—*Jack Ma's Quotations on Entrepreneurship,* 2008

CHINA IS FACING pressing issues such as a deteriorating environment and a widening wealth gap. If we cannot change our growth model, we could run into trouble. But only with a slower growth rate can China's economy change its course. It is easy for a small boat to change its course. But as the world's second-largest economy, China is like an ocean liner. We have to choose either to not slow down and overturn the ship, or slowing a bit to make the turn.

—*South China Morning Post*, April 21, 2016

We aim to foster an economy in which small business, young people and women in developing and under-developed nations can participate in and benefit from globalization.

—letter to shareholders, October 17, 2017

Donating money is important but not necessarily charitable. Donating that of which you have the least is real charity.

—*Jack Ma's Quotations on Entrepreneurship*, 2008

TECHNOLOGY DOES NOT have to be the culprit in widening the wealth gap around the world. I believe there is a massive opportunity to help alleviate poverty and catalyze economic development in China's rural countryside through technology and innovation.

—letter to shareholders, October 17, 2017

SPENDING MONEY IS more difficult than making money. Especially for philanthropy. When you have a good heart, you should also have good knowledge and good capability to spend the money, otherwise you are doing good thing with good heart with a terrible way.

—Stanford Graduate School of Business, September 24, 2015

WHAT WE WANT to build up is consciousness and awareness among people. We want people to take these issues seriously so that they think polluting is just as bad as committing a murder. Because, ultimately, it is. Business is important, but it is just as important to take action on these environmental issues as well.

I'm not an extremist. We're just taking a stand on what we believe is good for ourselves and our children. And I don't want people to do it merely because they are told it is a responsibility. I hate the word "responsibility." I am taking action because this is something I believe in. It is a way of thinking and a part of my philosophy.

—Nature.org, December 2009

Charity should not be done for publicity— it should be done quietly and anonymously.

—*Jack Ma's Quotations on Entrepreneurship*, 2008

It's too late
to complain,
"Whose fault?"
Whether
[climate change
is] your fault
or my fault,
let's solve
the problem
together.

—in conversation with President Barack Obama,
APEC CEO Summit, November 18, 2015

WHEN WE NEED too much, we destroy a lot
of things. . . . The past 200 years, because of
knowledge-based technology or knowledge-
based training systems, all we want to do
is get more. We want more things. We go
to the moon, we go to Mars. . . . We always
are looking. We human beings [are] never
inside looking. If you don't have the inside
looking, you will never be wise. If you are
not wise, you never know what you don't
want. Today, human beings get much more
than they expect they should have, so the
environmental pollutions, the whole thing
happening, is because human beings become
greedy.

—World Economic Forum, January 24, 2018

Part III

PERSONAL VALUES

Personal

THERE ARE THREE Jack Ma. First Jack Ma is people's imagination. Ahh, he's great, he's not good—this is the people's imagination. Second Jack Ma is Jack Ma as the CEO and the founder/chairman of Alibaba Group. And third Jack Ma is my real person. I love to sing, I love to dance, I have fun, I like walking around the streets.

—*Squawk Box,* December 5, 2017

I'M NOT GOOD at technology. I was trained to be a high school teacher. It's a funny thing. I'm running one of the biggest e-commerce companies in China, maybe in the world, but I know nothing about computers. All I know about computers is how to send and receive email and browse.

—**Asia Game Changer Awards ceremony, 2014**

I LOVE TAI chi. Tai chi is a philosophy. [It's] about yin and yang. Tai chi is about how you balance ... I use tai chi philosophy in business: calm down, there is always a way out, and keep yourself balanced. Competition is fun. Business is not like a battlefield where you die and I win. In business, even if you die, I may not win.

—World Economic Forum, January 23, 2015

I LEARNED MY English by myself when I was 12 years old, for whatever reason, I don't know—I just fell in love with the language. Every morning at five o'clock I rode a bicycle 40 minutes to the Hangzhou Hotel looking for foreign tourists to teach me English. I would show them around the city, and they would teach me English.

—Asia Game Changer Awards ceremony, 2014

I'm crazy, not stupid.

—*Jack Ma's Quotations on Entrepreneurship, 2008*

I can never be as rich as Bill Gates, but one thing I can do better than him, I can retire earlier than him.

—*Bloomberg*, September 6, 2018

IN THE PAST 15 years that I've been working, I've called myself "a blind man riding on the back of a blind tiger." Those experts riding horses, they all fell. We survived because we worried about the future. We believed in the future. We changed ourselves.

—Asia Game Changer Awards ceremony, 2014

FOR MY PERSONAL life, I don't want to die in the office. I want to die on the beach. I want to enjoy my life. Because we come to this world—not to work. We come to this world to enjoy life, make friends, have good families, and travel around the world.

—Fortune Global Forum, December 5, 2017

AS FOR MYSELF, I still have lots of dreams to pursue [after retirement]. Those who know me know that I do not like to sit idle. I plan on continuing my role as the founding partner in the Alibaba Partnership and contribute to the work of the partnership. I also want to return to education, which excites me with so much blessing because this is what I love to do. The world is big, and I am still young, so I want to try new things— because what if new dreams can be realized?!

—letter to customers, employees, and shareholders,
September 9, 2018

Leadership

CONTROL OF A company should never be about the number of shares a CEO holds. Rather, it should be about his or her wisdom and vision. Build your organization with a scientific, rational management team and don't allow any single investor or person full control.

—*Fortune Life Program*, March 29, 2003

WHEN YOU RUN a business, you need to be able to laugh, too. A strong vision and active mind allows for this. Take pride in what you do, and be capable and strong. To be able to laugh and be proud requires sharp eyes and a broad mind.

—Ningbo Network Operators Meeting, June 11, 2002

Hanging in my office as a reminder every day is a quote from martial arts novelist Jin Yong: "Great leaders know to treasure the talents around them."

—*Jiefang Daily*, September 4, 2008

IN OUR COMPANY, the organization chart is reversed. The client is on top, employees are right below them, then the managers, the vice presidents, and me, the CEO, at the bottom. My bosses are the vice presidents above me. The vice presidents' bosses are the managers above them—and so on up with employees having clients as their bosses. As CEO, I am the "goalkeeper" on this soccer team. If the goalkeeper sees the most action on the team, that means big trouble, no matter the skill level.

—Shenzhen Network Operators Meeting,
March 5, 2008

CHINESE BUSINESSES MUST pay great attention to team spirit. Cooperation comes from teamwork. Cast yourself as the singular hero above everyone else and suffer the consequences.

—Ningbo Network Operators Meeting,
June 11, 2002

Conduct yourself as a leader by being farsighted, broadminded, and capable and by working together with others. This is how I understand what it means to be a talented leader.

—Lakeside Academy, March 28, 2008

A GOOD LEADER grooms subordinates who can surpass them. It is all right to have them struggle in the process. If you can't find a suitable replacement within six months, then you have problems in recruiting good talent.

A leader should look for the best things inside each person. They should be able to find strengths in each that the person may be unaware of. Seeing and nurturing this potential is critical to your power as a leader. What made me think of this? Watching NBA games.

These basketball players get better because all 12 players on each team want to be on the court. All of them think they are good enough to play, and this produces a lot of peer pressure. If you have such a system in your company, where there are no guarantees but judgment is based on performance, you will field a good team.

—Ningbo Network Operators Meeting, June 11, 2002

THE ART OF being a leader is nothing but three things: vision, heart, and strength. Vision allows you to learn more by traveling a thousand miles than by reading a thousand books. Learning as you go from what you observe will enable you to see farther than others. Inside your town, you might already be the most powerful. Then you go to Shanghai and encounter others further along than you. Go on to Tokyo and New York and the number of powerful people seems endless. Therefore, as your vision broadens, others will come to admire you. A leader must also have heart. Nine out of ten very talented people are eccentric. Their unique temperament already has them thinking that they are the best at what they do. Tolerate them. Your heart needs to be expanded and will be if you are self-disciplined in this way every day. Some people are very funny, sitting and sulking over trifles. They make themselves miserable because they lack heart.

—*Fortune Life Program*, March 29, 2003

OF COURSE ALIBABA has faced its share of crises! How else could I possibly remain this thin and not gain even one kilo these past five years? I once thought when your company starts to grow the boss can relax a little. Instead, I'm more tired than ever! An entrepreneur constantly confronts crises— a good thing. Better to deal daily with small pains inside the company before they turn into a cancer.

—Hangzhou Network Operators Meeting,
September 15, 2007

IN BATTLE, SOLDIERS should not have binoculars. Otherwise, when the commander orders an assault, the soldiers might think, "Oh crap, we can see they have three machine guns, maybe we should retreat."

—*Jack Ma's Quotations on Entrepreneurship*, 2008

THE DAY YOU become a leader, you will be very lonely. Even the second- and third-in-command will find it difficult to understand you well.

When the captain sets sail, sometimes he personally climbs up the ship's pole to see which way the wind is blowing. For myself, I need to think of things a year ahead of time, to consider the right systems and deployment of human resources to come. Success may be another year off, so decisions now may not be clear until then. But I can't enjoy success unless I'm willing to shoulder the responsibility of failure.

—Shenzhen Network Operators Meeting,
March 5, 2008

You ACT AS a CEO only under two circumstances, neither during "normal" times. First, when you make a decision, and second, when you make mistakes. Always admit your mistakes and never look to find fault with your employees' execution or to blame your subordinates. A CEO shouldn't be preoccupied with claiming "success."

—Shenzhen Network Operators Meeting, March 5, 2008

As a leader, a CEO's education must include getting out to see the world and thinking about what he observes. . . . This is the way to bring opportunity and fortune to clients.

—Hangzhou Network Operators Meeting,
September 15, 2007

ANOTHER FUNCTION OF a leader is to discover the unique skills in every member of his team. In this world, there are no bad employees, only bad leaders and bad systems. Nurture carefully every worker's potential without exhausting it. . . . In the eyes of a leader, all employees are good. In the eyes of a professional manager, all are bad. A leader finds and utilizes the potential in all employees.

—Shanghai Network Operators Meeting, July 2005

LAST YEAR, I sent four colleagues back for their MBAs—one to Harvard and three to Wharton. I told them, "When you return and have forgotten all that the MBA program taught you, then you'll have graduated. However, if you're still caught up in all the rules and regulations, you'll need to continue your studies. After two years pursuing an MBA, you need at least half a year to forget what you learned. That's real success."

—World Economic Forum's China Business Summit,
April 19, 2002

Success and Failure

THE LESSONS I learned from the dark days at Alibaba are that you've got to make your team have value, innovation, and vision. Also, if you don't give up, you still have a chance. And, when you are small, you have to be very focused and rely on your brain, not your strength.

—*Inc.*, **January 1, 2008**

ACTUALLY, IT'S VERY easy to create a business. It's like walking in the dark, looking for light somewhere to guide you along. Only after 10 years am I comfortable now to talk about strategy and tactics. I prefer studying the reasons why businesses fail rather than why they succeed. People say that Jack Ma's leadership is the reason for Alibaba's survival. That's incorrect. I'm not that smart, but I am good at learning from experience.

—**Guangzhou Network Operators Meeting, March 21, 2005**

There is no CEO who does not make mistakes. Every successful person has faced frustration and made mistakes.

—Qingdao Network Operators Meeting,
July 22, 2005

THIS IS THE secret sauce of Alibaba: we
see the future . . . [and] not only see the
opportunity, but also see the disaster. When
the disaster comes, you know how to avoid it,
how to make use of it, and how to benefit.

—Alibaba Investor Day, September 18, 2018

IF A PERSON wants to be successful, he
should have a high EQ. But if you don't want
to lose quickly, you should have a high IQ.
But if you want to be respected, you should
have high LQ, the Q of love. So those three Qs
[should be] put together. A lot of men, they
have a high IQ, but low EQ, a very tiny LQ.
Women, balancewise, they are the best.

—World Economic Forum, January 24, 2018

THERE IS STILL a sizable gap between our top Chinese companies and large international firms. But while Western culture looks to big enterprise, here our 1.3 billion "ants" come from small- and medium-sized companies. This is where the victorious future lays, an army of Chinese network operators in small- to medium-sized firms besting big businesses. Be careful, then, in setting goals. If we set an unrealistic goal of a billion dollars in sales by tomorrow, we'll tire ourselves out in an atmosphere of failure. But if the goal is to run our company in a first-class manner without fixating on unrealistic numbers, we can have an army of 1.3 billion ants, clear-headed and ready to take on big elephants forever.

—Hangzhou Network Operators Meeting,
June 13, 2004

Four qualities
are needed along
with talent:
trustworthiness,
team spirit,
adaptability,
and optimism.

—*First Financial Daily,*
November 24, 2005

WHAT'S MOST IMPORTANT for a company's development in the 21st century? Employees. Treat them with respect and morale is greatly enhanced. Employee satisfaction ties directly into a company's prospects.

—Guangzhou Network Operators Meeting, March 21, 2005

E-COMMERCE CAN OFFER great contributions to the future, but there will be a crisis now and then. While it can be painful today and even more painful tomorrow, it can be beautiful the day after tomorrow. Keep on and hold on and always be ready for the worst that may happen tomorrow. Then you'll get to see the sun rise the day after tomorrow.

—press conference for Hong Kong Stock Exchange IPO listing, November 6, 2007

I don't know anything about computers so, as I often say to the younger generation, "If Jack Ma can succeed, then 80 percent of you can too by working hard."

—*Fortune Life Program*, March 29, 2003

I AM NOT the most talented person. My appearance, abilities, and education are far from society's best. But I understand human nature. You must control the negative and build up the positive to attain success. I try to do this through team spirit and shared missions.

—dialogue with Kazuo Inamori, October 28, 2008

WHETHER YOU ARE a big company or great company [doesn't] depend on what kind of opportunity you catch. Most of the companies in China, they are always waiting for opportunity. If there is a good opportunity, they catch it, they become a good company. When they miss some opportunities, they are gone. . . . I think that it's not about what kind of opportunities you grasp, it's about what kind of value you create for the future.

—Alibaba Investor Day, June 8, 2017

If you only regret the fact you failed but not the reasons for it, you'll always be in a state of regret.

—*Jack Ma's Quotations on Entrepreneurship*, 2008

FAILURE IN A fast-moving Internet company, no matter whether you call it a brain freeze or a brain fever, comes from fear of making mistakes. Mistakes have to be made today in order to grow and run better tomorrow. Just don't keep making the same mistake!

—Alibaba's 2nd anniversary celebration, September 10, 2001

STRENGTH ACCUMULATES FROM failure. If someday I brag to my grandchild all about my fine achievements, he or she may simply say, "What's so great about that? You simply rode the swelling Internet commerce tide in and found some investment." But if I talk about all my failures and mistakes in those years, then he or she may look at me with admiration. Final success includes many miserable experiences.

—Ningbo Network Operators Meeting, June 11, 2002

In 1999, Alibaba's early strategy was to skip over our domestic e-commerce market and immediately go international. We called this "jumping over a First Division Group A team to enter directly into the World Cup." However, from 1999 to 2001, Alibaba was not well known. Our focus was Europe and the United States, and I made many speeches over there then. My most miserable moment was at an event we organized in Germany in 2000. We set seats up for 1,500 people—only three showed up! I was very embarrassed but still had to go through with my speech.

—Qingdao Network Operators Meeting, July 22, 2005

WHEN DISASTER STRIKES, think of your clients. Then think of your employees and, after that, your competition. Actually, better not think about the competition because you need to handle your own troubles first. In dealing with a crisis, think of how it affects your clients and then your employees. If your employees are clear about how to react correctly, your survival for the long term is enhanced.

—*Win in China*, August 2007

Life
Lessons

Always keep
in mind these
three principles:
what you want
to do, what you
should do, and
for how long you
should do it.

—Beijing Network Operators Meeting,
March 17, 2008

THE THIRD WORLD war is going to happen,
and this war is not between nations. In this
war, we work together against the disease,
the poverty, the climate change—and I
believe this is our future. That human beings,
that nations, should unite together.

—Economic Club of New York, June 9, 2015

IF CHINA [KEEPS its] 9 percent growth of the
economy, there must be something wrong.
You will never see the blue sky. You will never
see the quality. China should pay attention
to the quality of the economy. . . . I think
[it's] just like a human grows. This body can
never [keep growing]. [At a] certain time, the
growth of the body will slow. [Instead, you]
should grow your mind, grow your culture,
grow your value, grow your wisdom. I think
China is moving to that direction.

—World Economic Forum, January 23, 2015

WHEN YOU ARE 20 to 30 years old, you
should follow a good boss, join a good
company to learn how to do things properly.
When you're 30 to 40 years old, if you want
to do something yourself, just do it. You still
can afford to lose, to fail. But when you're
40 to 50 years old, my suggestion is that
you should do things that you are good at,
all right, and not do things that, oh, that's
very interesting, I want to try something
new. It'll be dangerous more. When you're
50 to 60 years old, spend time training and
developing people of the next generation.
When you're over 60 years old, better stay
with your grandchildren.

—**World Economic Forum, January 24, 2018**

Pay attention to your own development and keep learning constantly. Never blame God or others for your position in life. Blame yourself.

—Shanghai Network Operators Meeting, July 2005

Never envy another big company. Your current company is the best as long as you share common goals, missions, and values.

—Shanghai Network Operators Meeting, July 2005

BE FIRM IN your beliefs. Hold on to them, study them, and do the right thing by them. These four key points guided Alibaba's early steps. Without this faith, you cannot walk. My firm belief was that the Internet would influence and change China, that China would develop e-commerce, and that e-commerce would help make its users rich.

—Hangzhou Network Operators Meeting, September 15, 2007

WESTERN CULTURE IS more knowledge-focused. It is inquisitive and acquisitive. Acquiring knowledge makes you smarter and makes you more capable of creating and acquiring material goods. Eastern culture is more wisdom-focused. The stress is on understanding what your essence is and to unburden yourself from the non-essentials.

—*South China Morning Post*, April 21, 2016

ALL THE THINGS we teach our kids today are how to remember more things, calculate faster—all these things machines will do better. Next 30 years, what are the things we should teach our kids, that they will be different, they can do better, they can do the things the machine cannot do? . . . I think we should teach our kids how to be more innovative, how to be more creative, and how to be more constructive.

—Tel Aviv University, May 3, 2018

MY FIRST OCCUPATION was teaching. If I can't now share my more than 10 years of entrepreneurial management experience with others, it'll be a waste. The more there is to share, the more to value and be treasured.

—dialogue with Kazuo Inamori, October 28, 2008

What's the difference between smart and wisdom? Smart people know what they want. Wise people know what they don't want.

—Global Engagement & Empowerment Forum, February 7, 2018

Machine is good [at] knowledge, but human beings are good at wisdom.

—CNBC, June 21, 2017

EVERYTHING I TAUGHT my students are the things I learned from books. So if I go and build up something and then go back, I can be a better teacher. This is my original thinking. I never thought I would be rich.

—University of Nairobi, July 20, 2017

As A TEACHER, you always believe in the future. You believe knowledge will change people's lives. You believe and you hope that your students are better than you are. Students are the best prize. Today I'm not a teacher, but I call CEO the "chief education officer" of my school.

—Asia Game Changer Awards ceremony, 2014

In the past 30 years, we make people like machine. Next 30 years, we will make machine like people.

—Bloomberg Global Business Forum, September 20, 2017

CONFIRM WHAT SHOULD be done to realize your dream. Often this involves taking a step back and letting something go. And be ready to give back and share with others at crucial moments.

—Shenzhen Network Operators Meeting,
March 5, 2008

WHAT I LIKE about Hollywood movies is the hero. In Chinese movies, we also have heroes, but all the heroes in Chinese movies die. In American movies all the heroes survive. So I ask people, if all the heroes die, who wants to be the heroes?

—*Bloomberg Markets*, November 11, 2015

The long distance needed to reach your goal isn't the problem. The problem is not knowing just how far that distance is.

—Ningbo Network Operators Meeting,
June 11, 2002

STUDENTS LIKE MY style. I believe that young people here are the same as me and like to hear the truth. I am thoroughly frank and honest with them. While telling the truth can be the most difficult thing in the world, it can also be the easiest. And when you tell the truth, people listen. When I criticize certain people it's because I love them. If they deserve criticism and I say nothing, it's because I don't like them.

—*Fortune Life Program*, March 29, 2003

MANY YEARS AGO, I wanted to change the world. Now I think if we want to change the world we must change ourselves. Changing ourselves is more important and easier than changing the world. Second, I want to improve the world. Changing the world— maybe that's Obama's job.

—World Economic Forum, January 23, 2015

FIVE YEARS AGO, my colleagues and I wanted to create the world's greatest company. Many thought such talk was mad. But no matter what was said, my dream to create such a company didn't change.

In the Internet recession of 2001–02 we talked only about "surviving." Even if all the other Internet companies died, we had to survive. And we did so only by refusing to give up, by believing in our dream. This incessant effort and constant ability to learn from our mistakes led to success. While today is tough, tomorrow can be even tougher. However, the day after tomorrow may be beautiful. But too many will give up after tough times on the eve of tomorrow. Therefore, never give up today!

—receiving **Economic Person of the Year in China Award,**
December 28, 2004

Milestones

1964

- Jack Ma is born in Hangzhou, Zhejiang Province, China, to two traditional Chinese storytellers.

1985

- Ma visits a friend in Australia, where he realizes that the world is much different than what he was taught in school.

1988

- Ma graduates from the Hangzhou Teacher's Institute with a bachelor's degree in English.

1995

- Ma visits Seattle, where his friend introduces him to the Internet.

- Ma, his wife Zang Ying, and a friend raise ¥20,000 and launch China Yellow Pages, a web development company.

1998

- Jack Ma and the other 17 founders prepare to create China's first online trading market.

1999

- Alibaba Group launches its website, a B2B e-commerce platform, in March.

- Alibaba Group absorbs a USD$5 million venture capital fund led by Goldman Sachs and other first-class fund companies in the United States, Asia, and Europe.

2000

- Alibaba Group raises USD$20 million from investors such as SoftBank, Goldman Sachs, and Fidelity.

- Alibaba Group holds the first West Lake Summit, a forum for Internet-business leaders.

2001

- Alibaba Group launches TrustPass in order to better serve their international sellers.

- Registered users exceeds 1 million, making Alibaba Group the world's first e-commerce website with more than 1 million members.

2002

- Alibaba Group turns a profit for the first time.

2003

- Alibaba Group invests ¥450 million to create and launch Taobao, a C2C e-commerce platform.

- Alibaba Group introduces the communication software AliTalk, which allows buyers and sellers to communicate instantly online.

- Alibaba Group creates Alipay, an independent, secure online payment service on Taobao's platform.

2004

- Alibaba Group receives USD$82 million from investment institutions such as SoftBank, Fidelity Investment, DFJ, and Granite, becoming the biggest private equity investment in a Chinese Internet company.

- Alibaba Group hosts the first Netreprenuer Summit.

- Alibaba Group launches Aliwangwang, an instant messaging tool, on Taobao.

- Alipay becomes a separate company.

- Jack Ma is named one of CCTV's Top 10 Business Leaders of the Year.

2005

- Yahoo! purchases a 40 percent stake in Alibaba Group, investing USD$1 billion.

- Alibaba Group takes over control of China Yahoo!.

- Alibaba Group is chosen as the best employer in the annual CCTV Employer of the Year survey.

- Alibaba Group pays a daily tax of ¥1 million to the government, one of the highest in China. This is a point of pride for Jack Ma, as it demonstrates the size and growth of his company.

- *Businessweek* names Jack Ma "Businessperson of the Year."

2006

- Taobao battles eBay for e-commerce dominance in China and wins—eBay shuts down its site in China.

2007

- Alibaba Group launches the Taobao University program for e-commerce users.

- The Hangzhou People's Government, Chinese E-Commerce Association, and Alibaba Group jointly organize and hold the Second Network Operators Festival in Hangzhou.

- Alibaba.com is successfully listed on the main board of the Stock Exchange of Hong Kong in November for HK$13.1 billion (USD$1.7 billion), making the company the second-largest global IPO for an Internet company.

- Alibaba Group launches Alimama, an online marketing platform.

2008

- Taobao holds its fifth anniversary celebration, and Ma announces an investment of ¥2 billion in the Taobao website.

- Taoboa launches Taobao Mall (TMall.com), a business-to-consumer retail website.

- Alibaba Group launches the Alibaba Group R&D Institute.

2009

- Alibaba Group celebrates its 10th anniversary.

- Jack Ma creates Singles Day.

- Alipay surpasses 200 million users, which means that more than half of Chinese netizens use e-commerce.

- General Atlantic, a global growth-equity firm, invests USD$75 million in Alibaba Group.

- Alibaba Group launches Alibaba Cloud Computing (AliCloud).

- Alibaba.com buys HiChina, the country's biggest Internet service provider.

- Ma is listed by *Time* in its list of the world's 100 most influential people.

- Ma is named one of CCTV's Economic People of the Year: Business Leaders of the Decade.

2010

- Alibaba.com is renamed 1688.com

- Alibaba Group launches AliExpress, which facilitates Chinese exports.

- Alibaba Group announces an executive committee to spearhead the "Big Taobao" strategy, an effort to aggregate Alibaba companies and subsidiaries. The members are the executives from Taobao, Alipay, Alibaba Cloud Computing, and China Yahoo!.

- Alibaba Group announces that it will appropriate 0.3 percent of annual revenues to an environmental protection fund to promote awareness about the environment.

- Alibaba Group purchases Vendio and Auctiva, e-commerce service providers for US small businesses.

- Taobao launches its mobile app.

2011

- Tmall.com becomes an independent company.

- Alibaba announces a warehousing network system in China and invests heavily in the Chinese logistics industry.

- The SEC files submitted by Yahoo! reveal that Ma transferred Alipay ownership under the Alibaba Group to a domestically funded company (Alibaba Zhejiang), which is held by Ma and Xie Shihuang, one of Alibaba's founders. The battle to control Alipay emerges.

- Alipay is authorized by the People's Bank of China and obtains a third-party pay license. It was one of the first 27 companies approved for this license.

- Alibaba Group, Yahoo!, and SoftBank officially sign an agreement regarding the transfer of Alipay equity. Alipay continues to provide services to the Alibaba Group and its relevant companies, but Alibaba will also receive reasonable economic returns given by Alipay Holding Company.

- Jack Ma clearly expresses his intention to acquire Yahoo! shares.

- Alibaba Group and Yahoo! jointly announce that both parties have signed the final agreement regarding the equity repurchase. Alibaba spends USD$7.1 billion to repurchase 20 percent equity from Yahoo!.

- Alibaba Network Co., Ltd. is officially unlisted from the Hong Kong Stock Exchange.

2012

- Alibaba Group creates the Alibaba Foundation, which funds social causes.

- Alibaba Group completes the preliminary equity repurchase from Yahoo! and restructures their relationship.

- The Taobao website and TMall platform break ¥1 trillion in turnover.

MILESTONES

2013

- Taobao celebrates its 10th anniversary.

- Jack Ma announces to employees that he is stepping down as CEO of the Alibaba Group.

- Jonathan Lu becomes Alibaba's CEO and Ma stays on as executive chairman.

- Alibaba Group launches Alibaba Smart TV OS and Laiwang, a social networking app.

- In November, Ma is awarded an honorary doctoral degree from the Hong Kong University of Science and Technology.

- Alibaba Group partners with private corporations such as Yintai Group, Shunfeng Group, Zhongtong, Yuantong, Shentong, and Yunda, to establish Rookie Internet Technology Co., Ltd. and starts the project construction of the Chinese Wisdom Backbone Network (CSN). Ma is named chairman.

- Alibaba Group becomes a shareholder of ShopRunner, an American e-commerce, logistics, and distribution service that is owned by eBay. Alibaba takes the lead in second-round financing of ShopRunner, purchasing 30 percent of shares.

- Singles Day brings in 170 million Alipay transactions for a total of ¥35 billion in revenue, an increase of 83 percent compared to the previous year's ¥19.1 billion.

- *Forbes* ranks Jack Ma 30th on its World's Most Powerful People list.

2014

- Jack Ma and Joe Tsai, a cofounder of Alibaba Group, announce the Personal Public Welfare Trust Fund. This fund comes from their options in Alibaba and represents about 2 percent of the Alibaba Group's total shares.

- Alibaba Group acquires a 60 percent stake in China-Vision, a film and television production company.

- Alibaba (BABA) begins trading on the New York Stock Exchange at USD$68 a share. At USD$21.8 billion, it is the biggest IPO in history.

- The Alibaba Group's market value reaches USD$238.332 billion, and Ma's net worth reaches USD$21.212 billion, making him one of the richest people in the world.

- *Time* includes Jack Ma on its annual list of most influential people.

- Alibaba Group purchases a significant stake in Youku Tudou, which is similar to YouTube but operates in China.

- Alibaba Group launches Ali Health, an e-commerce platform that specializes in pharmaceuticals, health products, and medical services.

- Alibaba Group purchases a 50 percent stake in the Guangzhou Evergrande Football Club for USD$192 billion.

- Ma receives the Asia Society's Asia Game Changer of the Year Award.

2015

- *Forbes* names Ma the 22nd most powerful man in the world.

- Singles Day (November 11) generates USD$14.32 billion for Alibaba, a 60 percent increase from the previous year.

- Alibaba enters India's e-commerce space by acquiring a 25 percent stake in Paytm owner One97 Communications.

- Alibaba acquires the *South China Morning Post* and its assets for USD$266 million.

2016

- Jack Ma first proposes the idea of the Electronic World Trade Platform (eWTP), a private-sector initiative to promote global Internet-based trade.

- Alibaba agrees to acquire a controlling stake in the Southeast Asian e-commerce platform Lazada.

- In partnership with SAIC Motor Corp., Alibaba introduces the OS'Car, the first mass-produced Internet car.

- Alibaba Group acquires a stake in Steven Spielberg's production company, Amblin Partners.

- Ma joins the board of Breakthrough Energy Ventures, Bill Gates's investment fund for new energy technologies.

2017

- Ma meets with President Donald Trump to discuss how to create 1 million jobs in the United States within five years.

- Alibaba Group uses its Gateway '17 conference in Toronto to educate farmers and businesses on how to use Alibaba's Tmall program to sell goods to China and create jobs in the United States and Canada.

- In May, Alibaba officially breaks the USD$300 billion valuation mark and then, two months later in July, breaks the USD$400 billion valuation mark, becoming the first Asian company to do so.

- Alibaba Group launches Alibaba DAMO Academy, an international research program with the goal of advancing understanding of machine learning, data intelligence, quantum computing, and many other cutting-edge research areas.

- Ma makes his acting debut in the kung fu short film *Gong Shou Dao*.

- *Forbes* ranks Ma second on its 2017 World's Greatest Leaders list.

- Alibaba Group launches the Alibaba Poverty Relief Fund, a philanthropic effort that focuses on education, women's empowerment, and environmental protection.

2018

- Ma creates the Netrepreneur Prize, a USD$10 million investing fund for entrepreneurs in Africa.

- In September, Ma announces he will retire from his position as chairman of Alibaba Group in September 2019, with Alibaba CEO Daniel Zhang stepping in to replace him.

- In an interview with Chinese news agency Xinhua, Ma steps back his plans to create 1 million jobs in the United States. He states that the escalating trade conflict between China and the United States makes the promise impossible to keep.

- On September 19, 2018, Mr. Zhang Jianfeng, CTO of Alibaba announces that the company will establish Pingtouge Semiconductor Co., Ltd., which makes Alibaba the fifth largest technology enterprise in the world in quantum hardware R&D projects after IBM, Microsoft, Google and Intel.

- In October, ISO/IEC JTC1 SC27 officially passes the Alibaba-led Inernational Standards Project on Big Data Security and Privacy, which means Alibaba's data security technology and management experience will be expected to become an international standard for global data security management.

Acknowledgments

From Bob Song: I am very proud that this second edition is being launched in the United States. I appreciate my sister, Suk Lee's, great idea and offer to work on this book together. She is a very unique voice in American publishing, given her global perspective and experience. Compared to five years ago, the world has changed a lot. But whatever the changes, America and China should better understand each other. Jack Ma is a very special example to prove one thing: that good cooperation is always better than a bad trade war. Enjoy!

From Suk Lee: In addition, we thank our publisher, Doug Seibold, our editor, Jessica Easto, and our publicist at Agate, Jacqueline Jarik, for guiding us through our first book. They have made this book possible.

About the Editors

Suk Lee is a publishing veteran who has worked for many major American publishers. She graduated from New York University with a degree in English Literature. She lives in New York City.

Bob Song is a Chinese publishing and IT industry veteran. He lives in Beijing.